Terezín *and* Theresienstadt

CONCENTRATION CAMP AND GHETTO

A TRAVEL PHOTO ART BOOK

LAINE CUNNINGHAM

Terezín and Theresienstadt

Concentration Camp and Ghetto

A Travel Photo Art Book

Published by Sun Dogs Creations
Changing the World One Book at a Time
Print ISBN: 9781946732965

Cover Design by Angel Leya

Copyright © 2019 Laine Cunningham

All rights reserved. No part of this book may be reproduced in any form or by any means, electronic, mechanical, digital, photocopying or recording, except for the inclusion in a review, without permission in writing from the publisher.

THE TRAVEL PHOTO ART SERIES

Bikes of Berlin
Necropolises of New Orleans I & II
Ruins of Rome I & II
Ancients of Assisi I & II
Panoramas of Portugal
Nuances of New York
Glimpses of Germany
Impressions of Italy
Altitudes of the Alps
Knights Through the Ages
Coast of California
Utopia of the Unicorn
Flourishes of France
Portraits of Paris
Tableaus of Tbilisi
Grandeur in the Republic of Georgia
Paragons of Prague
Hidden Prague
Lidice Lives
Along the Via Appia
The Pillars of the Bohemian Paradise
Terezín and Theresienstadt

SHIELD OF DAVID

PARTED

Terezín, widely known as the Theresienstadt concentration camp, is a centuries-old compound in the Czech Republic. Habsburg emperor Joseph II ordered the compound built. Construction took place from 1780 to 1790 as a way to defend the bridges at the Ohře and Elbe Rivers against Prussian soldiers invading Bohemia.

BEHIND THE GATE

SOLITARY

Once finished, Terezín could hold as many as 11,000 soldiers. When the First World War exploded in Europe, the fortress became a prison camp for thousands of political criminals. Gavrilo Princip, the assassin of Archduke Franz Ferdinand and his wife, was imprisoned there until his death in 1918.

World War II brought the unwilling annexation of Sudetenland, a number of Czechoslovakia's border districts, by Germany during the Munich Agreement. Only a year later, in 1939, the rest of Bohemia and Moravia had been occupied.

PLACING THE STONE

The Gestapo transformed Terezín into Theresienstadt, a ghetto and concentration camp. Jews from Czechoslovakia were imprisoned there along with tens of thousands of Jewish individuals deported from Germany and Austria. Hundreds arrived from the Netherlands and Denmark.

SEVEL

LIES

A number of individuals arrived willingly. They had been told they would be taken to a retirement home where all their needs would be tended. After signing over their wealth, they were transported instead to the ghetto.

HIDDEN

Annual visits from officials charged with ensuring the conditions were humane were said to be insufficient, if not corrupt. Lax oversight combined with false facilities turned Theresienstadt into the hell the Reich had intended.

IRON

Theresienstadt was not an extermination camp. Instead, overcrowding, disease, and poor nutrition at the camp killed some 33,000 prisoners. Of the 150,000 Jewish people sent there, 15,000 were children.

SHUTTERED

VEIL

Despite these torments, the prisoners formed a community. Theresienstadt has become known for its rich cultural life. Concerts, lectures, and youth education continued under the purview of a Jewish governing group. The Ghetto Central Library grew to over 100,000 volumes. Artists Bedřich Fritta, Norbert Troller, Leo Haas, Otto Ungar, and Petr Kien worked alongside conductor Karel Ančerl, cantor Karl Fischer, and composer Viktor Ullmann.

WITNESS

When the war ended,
Theresienstadt's survivors
numbered 17,247.

EL MALEI RACHAMIM

MEM

ABOUT THE AUTHOR

Laine Cunningham leads readers around the world. *The Family Made of Dust* is set in the Australian Outback, while *Reparation* is a novel of the American Great Plains. Her travel memoir *Woman Alone* appeals to fans of *Wild* and *Eat Pray Love*.

NOVELS BY LAINE CUNNINGHAM

The Family Made of Dust

Beloved

Reparation

OTHER BOOKS BY LAINE CUNNINGHAM

Woman Alone: A Six-Month Journey Through the Australian Outback

On the Wallaby Track

Seven Sisters: Spiritual Messages from Aboriginal Australia

Writing While Female or Black or Gay

The Zen of Travel
The Zen of Gardening
Zen in the Stable
The Zen of Chocolate
The Zen of Dogs

Bikes of Berlin
Necropolises of New Orleans I & II
Ruins of Rome I & II
Ancients of Assisi I & II
Panoramas of Portugal
Nuances of New York
Glimpses of Germany
Impressions of Italy
Altitudes of the Alps
Knights Through the Ages
Coast of California
Utopia of the Unicorn
Flourishes of France
Portraits of Paris
Tableaus of Tbilisi
Grandeur in the Republic of Georgia
Paragons of Prague
Hidden Prague
Lidice Lives
Along the Via Appia
The Pillars of the Bohemian Paradise
Terezín and Theresienstadt

The Wisdom of Puppies
The Wisdom of Babies
The Wisdom of Weddings

The Beautiful Book of Questions
The Beautiful Book for Dream Seekers
The Beautiful Book for Rebels
The Beautiful Book for Women
The Beautiful Book for Lovers

www.ingramcontent.com/pod-product-compliance
Lightning Source LLC
Chambersburg PA
CBHW041322110526
44591CB00021B/2877